The Story of
The Ten Commandments

As told by
Pastor Chuck Smith

WITH ILLUSTRATIONS BY JOHN SHAFFER

The Word For Today, P.O. Box 8000, Costa Mesa, CA 92628 • Web Site: www.twft.com • E-mail: info@twft.com

The Story of The Ten Commandments
By Chuck Smith
With illustrations by John Shaffer
Editing by Shannon Woodward

Published by The Word For Today
P.O. Box 8000, Costa Mesa, CA 92628
Web site: http://www.twft.com
(800) 272-WORD (9673)
© 2013 The Word For Today

ISBN: 978-1-59751-138-4

Scriptural quotations are based on the King James Version of the Bible. Translational emendations, amplifications and paraphrases are by the author.

Printed in the United States of America.

A special thanks to the following for their voice talent in the audio recording of this book:

- Sandy Adams
- Ray Bentley
- Cheryl Brodersen
- Gerry Brown
- Peggy Brown
- Joey Buran
- Bob Caldwell
- Nicolette Cook
- Tommy Cota
- Bob Coy
- Gayle Erwin
- William Funderburk
- Ken Graves
- David Guzik
- Ken Ham
- Bryan Jameson
- Pancho Juarez
- Toni Rich
- Billy Rutledge
- Shannon Shaffer
- Tom Stipe
- Christian Towgood
- Michelle Wright

DOES IT SEEM like there are a lot of rules in life? Well, God gave us only ten. He wrote them down for us on two stone tablets.

God gave those tablets to Moses, who had been born a Hebrew but he was raised in Pharaoh's household. To save his life, Moses' mother placed him in a basket and sent him down the river, and the Egyptian princess found him.

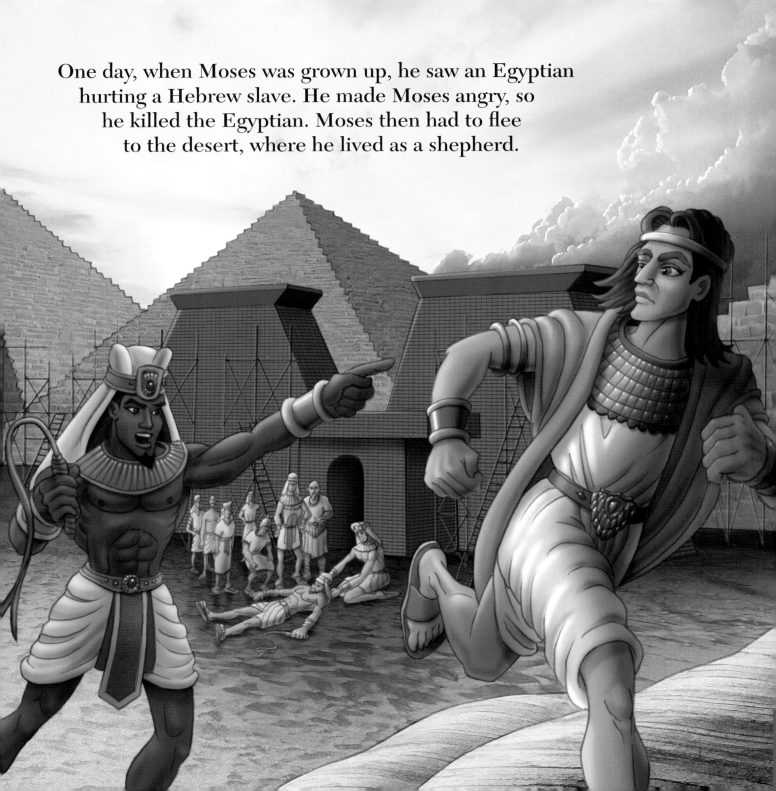

One day, when Moses was grown up, he saw an Egyptian
hurting a Hebrew slave. He made Moses angry, so
he killed the Egyptian. Moses then had to flee
to the desert, where he lived as a shepherd.

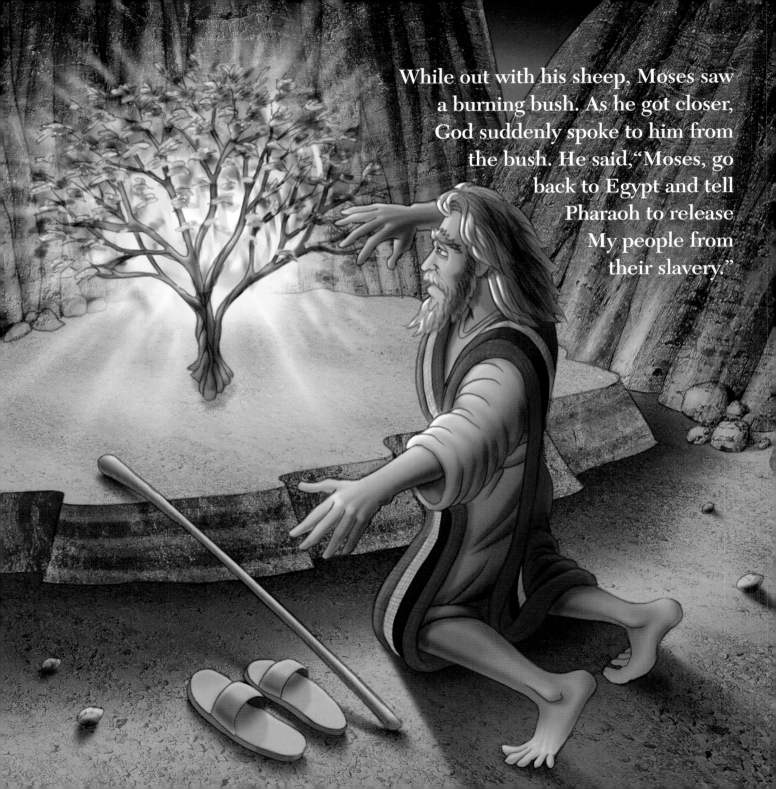

While out with his sheep, Moses saw a burning bush. As he got closer, God suddenly spoke to him from the bush. He said, "Moses, go back to Egypt and tell Pharaoh to release My people from their slavery."

So Moses went back to Egypt and told Pharaoh, "God wants you to let His people go so they can worship Him in their own land." But Pharaoh said no.

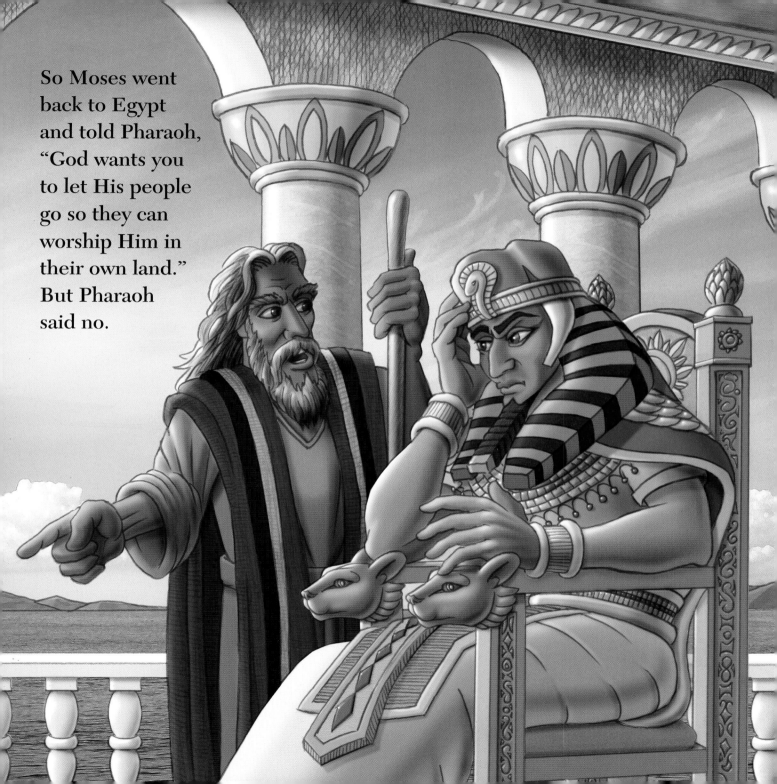

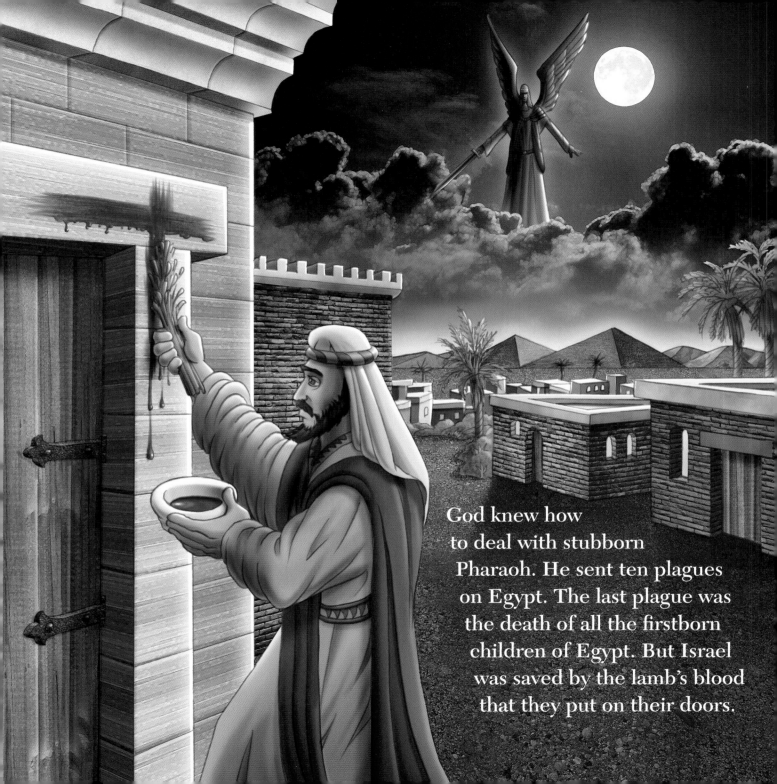

God knew how
to deal with stubborn
Pharaoh. He sent ten plagues
on Egypt. The last plague was
the death of all the firstborn
children of Egypt. But Israel
was saved by the lamb's blood
that they put on their doors.

When Pharaoh woke up the next morning, he saw how many Egyptians had died in the night. He finally let God's people go. So they packed up their belongings and they set off for the Promised Land.

Then Pharaoh changed his mind. He sent his army to chase the Israelites. But God held up the waters of the Red Sea so they could pass safely through … and then afterwards those waters swallowed up Pharaoh's army.

God took good care of the Israelites in the desert. He caused manna to fall from the sky every day to feed them. It was sweet and nourishing. And when they were thirsty, He made water come out from the rock.

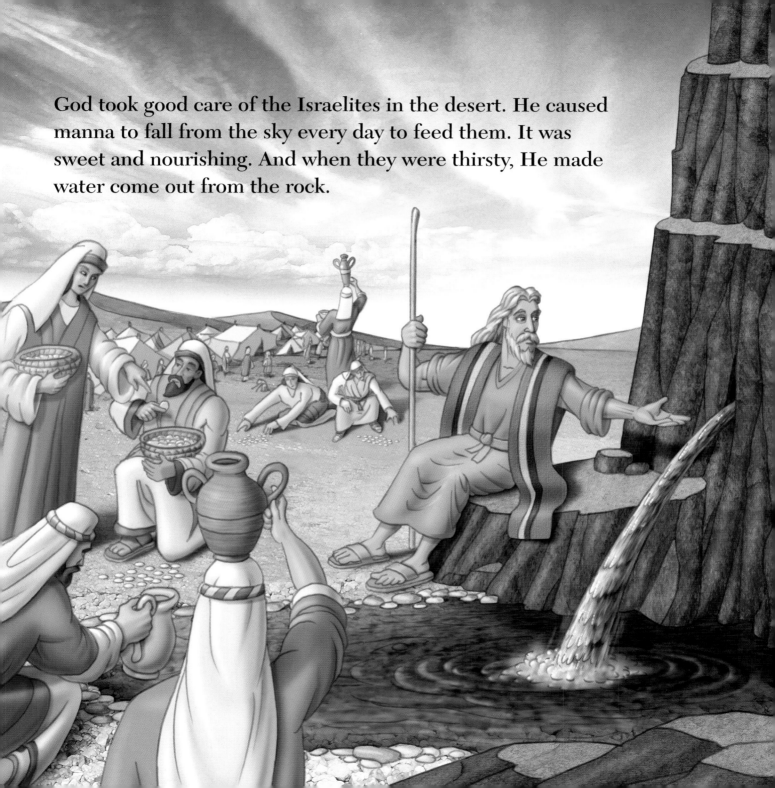

But the Israelites complained a lot. God sent serpents into the camp, and everyone who was bitten died. So God had Moses make a brass serpent and lift it up high. Those bitten were saved if they looked at the brass serpent.

One day, Moses went up the mountain to meet with God and He gave Moses ten rules for life. These Ten Commandments were engraved on two stone tablets.

1

I

YOU SHALL
HAVE NO OTHER
GODS BEFORE ME.

II

YOU SHALL NOT
MAKE FOR YOURSELF
A CARVED IMAGE.

III

YOU SHALL NOT TAKE
THE NAME OF THE LORD
YOUR GOD IN VAIN.

IV

REMEMBER THE
SABBATH DAY,
TO KEEP IT HOLY.

V

HONOR YOUR FATHER
AND YOUR MOTHER.

VI

YOU SHALL
NOT MURDER.

VII

YOU SHALL NOT
COMMIT ADULTERY.

VIII

YOU SHALL
NOT STEAL.

IX

YOU SHALL NOT BEAR
FALSE WITNESS AGAINST
YOUR NEIGHBOR.

X

YOU SHALL
NOT COVET.

You shall have no other gods before Me.

Whatever you love the most in life is your god. The first commandment tells us to love God more than anything else.

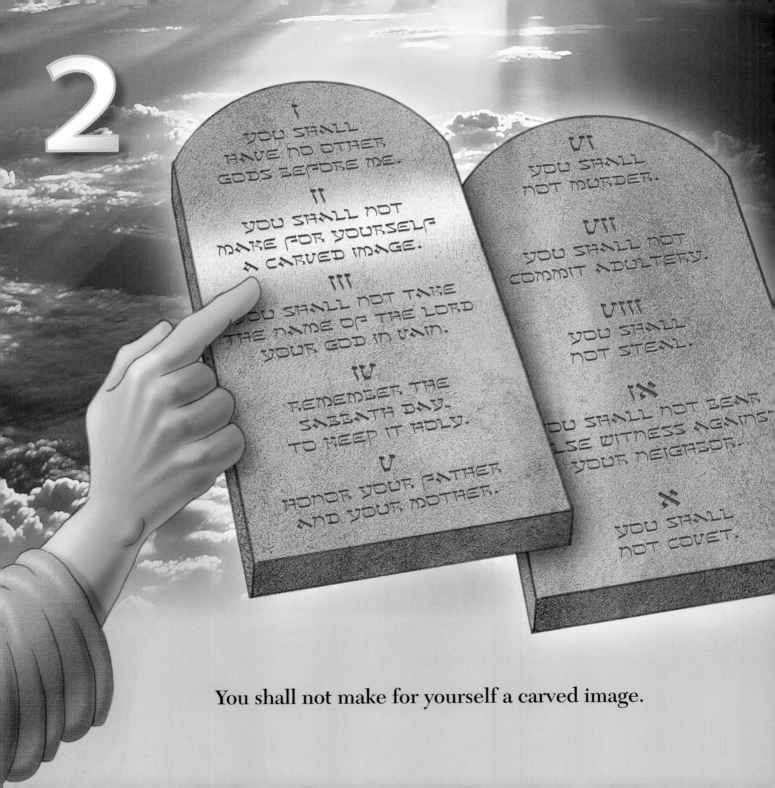

You shall not make for yourself a carved image.

All through the ages, people have made little images or idols that they worship. Those idols then become the most important things to the people. So God tells us, "Don't do it."

You shall not take the name of the Lord your God in vain.

Sometimes when people are surprised, or have hurt themselves, or they're mad, they say the Lord's name in a bad way. But God's name is to be respected. We must be careful to use His name the right way.

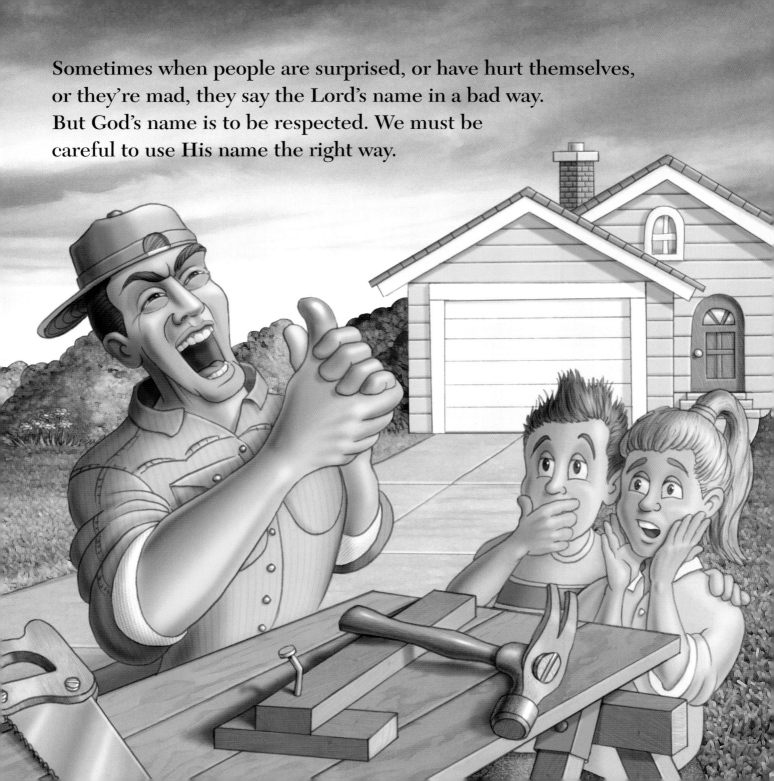

Remember the Sabbath Day to keep it holy.

Most people are busy all week long. God deserves one day a week when we leave our work behind and we gather at church to worship Him, learn about Him, and give Him a chance to speak to our hearts.

Honor your father and your mother.

God asks your parents to take care of you, and He asks you to respect and honor them. You can do that by listening to what they say and obeying what they ask you to do.

You shall not murder.

God is the one who gave us life.
We don't have the right to take
someone else's life just because
they hurt us or made us mad.

You shall not commit adultery.

When a man and a woman get married, they promise
to love, to cherish, and to stay true to one another.
God hears those promises and He expects
us to keep them. So we're not to get
interested in any other person.

You shall not steal.

Sometimes people are tempted to take what doesn't belong to them, and they say, "It's just a little thing. It won't matter." But whether it's a big thing or a little thing, God says, "It's all stealing. Don't do it."

You shall not bear false witness against your neighbor.

tell lies about other people. Anytime we speak falsely about someone else, we're hurting that person. So we're not to do it—not for any reason.

You shall not covet.

To covet is to want something that belongs to someone else, and to wish that it belonged to you. We need to be happy with what we have and trust that God will give us what we need.

GET YOURS TODAY!

DELUXE
Princess
CRUISER

God wants us to keep the
Ten Commandments, but we just
can't do it! So Jesus came and
did it for us. He paid the penalty
on the cross so that we can
be right with God.
Thank You, Jesus!

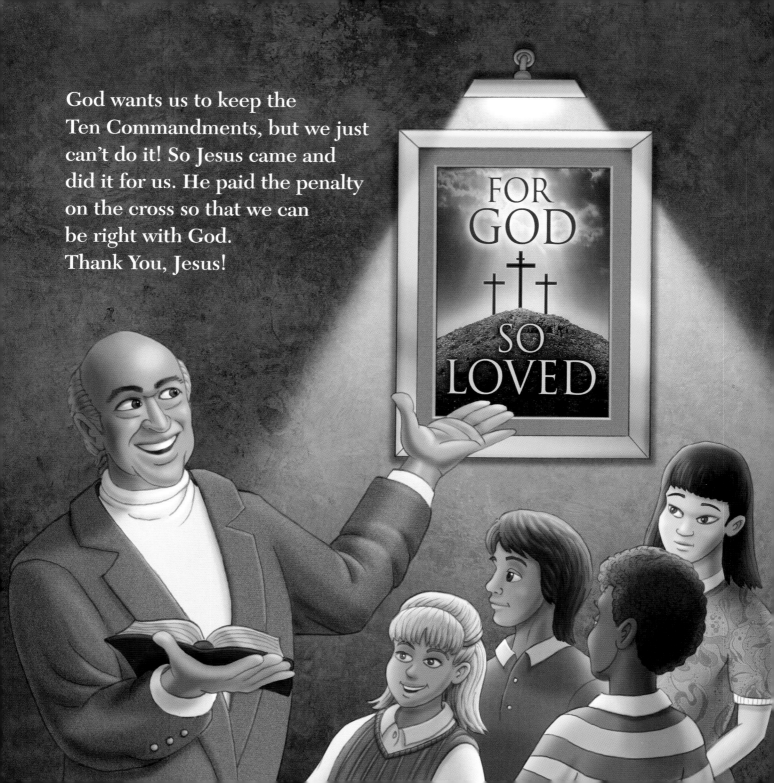

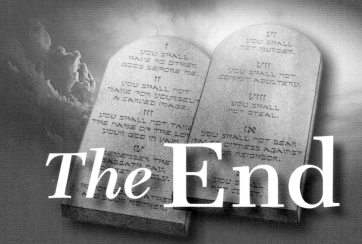

The End